Children's History of the World

THE

MEDIEVAL WORLD

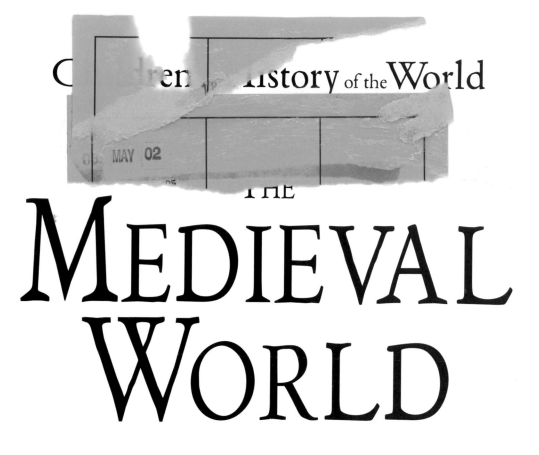

500 646 366 X2

OXFORD
Children's History of the World

THE
MEDIEVAL
WORLD

Neil Grant

OXFORD
UNIVERSITY PRESS

OXFORD

UNIVERSITY PRESS

Great Clarendon Street, Oxford OX2 6DP

Oxford University Press is a department of the University of Oxford.
It furthers the University's objective of excellence in research, scholarship,
and education by publishing worldwide in

Oxford New York

Athens Auckland Bangkok Bogotá Buenos Aires Kolkata
Cape Town Chennai Dar es Salaam Delhi Florence Hong Kong Istanbul
Karachi Kuala Lumpur Madrid Melbourne Mexico City Mumbai
Nairobi Paris São Paulo Shanghai Singapore Taipei Tokyo Toronto Warsaw

with associated companies in Berlin Ibadan

Oxford is a registered trade mark of Oxford University Press
in the UK and in certain other countries

Text copyright © Neil Grant 2001
Illustrations copyright © Oxford University Press 2001

The moral rights of the author/artist have been asserted

Database right Oxford University Press (maker)

First published 2001
Some material in this book was previously
published in Children's History of the World 2000

All rights reserved. No part of this publication may be reproduced,
stored in a retrieval system, or transmitted, in any form or by any means,
without the prior permission in writing of Oxford University Press.
Within the UK, exceptions are allowed in respect of any fair
dealing for the purpose of research or private study, or criticism or
review, as permitted under the Copyright, Designs and Patents Act 1988,
or in the case of reprographic reproduction in accordance with
the terms of the licences issued by the Copyright Licensing Agency.
Enquiries concerning reproduction outside these terms and in other
countries should be sent to the Rights Department, Oxford University Press,
at the address above.

This book is sold subject to the condition that it shall not, by way of trade or
otherwise, be lent, re-sold, hired out or otherwise circulated without the
publisher's prior consent in any form of binding or cover other than that in
which it is published and without a similar condition including this condition
being imposed on the subsequent purchaser.

500 646366

British Library Cataloguing in Publication Data available

Paperback ISBN 0-19-910823-4

1 3 5 7 9 10 8 6 4 2

Printed in Malaysia

CONSULTANTS
Mike Corbishley
Dr. Narayani Gupta
Dr. Rick Halpern
Dr. Douglas H. Johnson
Rosemary Kelly
James Mason

Contents

How to use this book

This book is divided into double-page spreads, each on a different subject. At the end of the book there is a Timeline. This shows at a glance the developments in different regions of the world during the period covered by the section. There is also a Who's Who page, which gives short biographies of the most important people of the period, a Glossary of important words, and an Index.

The title describes the subject of the spread, like a newspaper headline.

The first paragraph sets the scene, explaining what the spread is about and why it is important.

Fact boxes list key events associated with the subject.

Dates here show the time in history when the events took place.

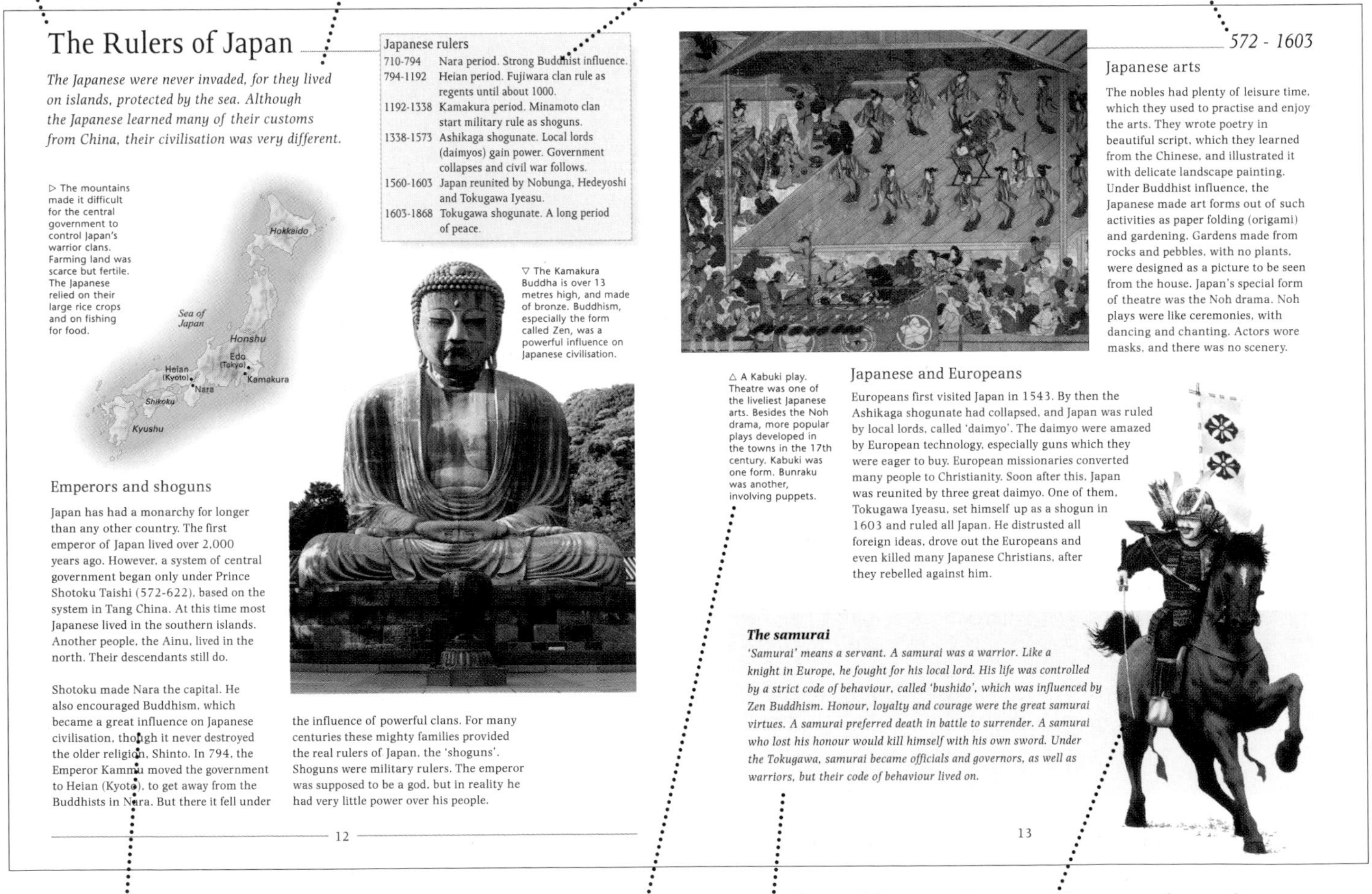

The Rulers of Japan

The Japanese were never invaded, for they lived on islands, protected by the sea. Although the Japanese learned many of their customs from China, their civilisation was very different.

Japanese rulers	
710-794	Nara period. Strong Buddhist influence.
794-1192	Heian period. Fujiwara clan rule as regents until about 1000.
1192-1338	Kamakura period. Minamoto clan start military rule as shoguns.
1338-1573	Ashikaga shogunate. Local lords (daimyos) gain power. Government collapses and civil war follows.
1560-1603	Japan reunited by Nobunga, Hedeyoshi and Tokugawa Iyeasu.
1603-1868	Tokugawa shogunate. A long period of peace.

▷ The mountains made it difficult for the central government to control Japan's warrior clans. Farming land was scarce but fertile. The Japanese relied on their large rice crops and on fishing for food.

▽ The Kamakura Buddha is over 13 metres high, and made of bronze. Buddhism, especially the form called Zen, was a powerful influence on Japanese civilisation.

Emperors and shoguns

Japan has had a monarchy for longer than any other country. The first emperor of Japan lived over 2,000 years ago. However, a system of central government began only under Prince Shotoku Taishi (572-622), based on the system in Tang China. At this time most Japanese lived in the southern islands. Another people, the Ainu, lived in the north. Their descendants still do.

Shotoku made Nara the capital. He also encouraged Buddhism, which became a great influence on Japanese civilisation, though it never destroyed the older religion, Shinto. In 794, the Emperor Kammu moved the government to Heian (Kyoto), to get away from the Buddhists in Nara. But there it fell under the influence of powerful clans. For many centuries these mighty families provided the real rulers of Japan, the 'shoguns'. Shoguns were military rulers. The emperor was supposed to be a god, but in reality he had very little power over his people.

12

572 - 1603

Japanese arts

The nobles had plenty of leisure time, which they used to practise and enjoy the arts. They wrote poetry in beautiful script, which they learned from the Chinese, and illustrated it with delicate landscape painting. Under Buddhist influence, the Japanese made art forms out of such activities as paper folding (origami) and gardening. Gardens made from rocks and pebbles, with no plants, were designed as a picture to be seen from the house. Japan's special form of theatre was the Noh drama. Noh plays were like ceremonies, with dancing and chanting. Actors wore masks, and there was no scenery.

△ A Kabuki play. Theatre was one of the liveliest Japanese arts. Besides the Noh drama, more popular plays developed in the towns in the 17th century. Kabuki was one form. Bunraku was another, involving puppets.

Japanese and Europeans

Europeans first visited Japan in 1543. By then the Ashikaga shogunate had collapsed, and Japan was ruled by local lords, called 'daimyo'. The daimyo were amazed by European technology, especially guns which they were eager to buy. European missionaries converted many people to Christianity. Soon after this, Japan was reunited by three great daimyo. One of them, Tokugawa Iyeasu, set himself up as a shogun in 1603 and ruled all Japan. He distrusted all foreign ideas, drove out the Europeans and even killed many Japanese Christians, after they rebelled against him.

The samurai

'Samurai' means a servant. A samurai was a warrior. Like a knight in Europe, he fought for his local lord. His life was controlled by a strict code of behaviour, called 'bushido', which was influenced by Zen Buddhism. Honour, loyalty and courage were the great samurai virtues. A samurai preferred death in battle to surrender. A samurai who lost his honour would kill himself with his own sword. Under the Tokugawa, samurai became officials and governors, as well as warriors, but their code of behaviour lived on.

13

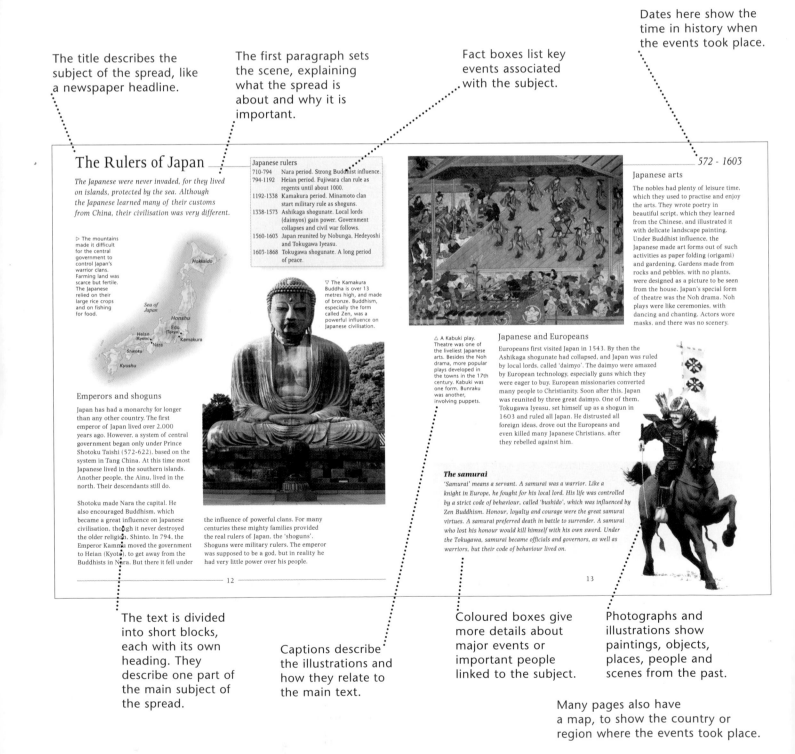

The text is divided into short blocks, each with its own heading. They describe one part of the main subject of the spread.

Captions describe the illustrations and how they relate to the main text.

Coloured boxes give more details about major events or important people linked to the subject.

Photographs and illustrations show paintings, objects, places, people and scenes from the past.

Many pages also have a map, to show the country or region where the events took place.

Introduction

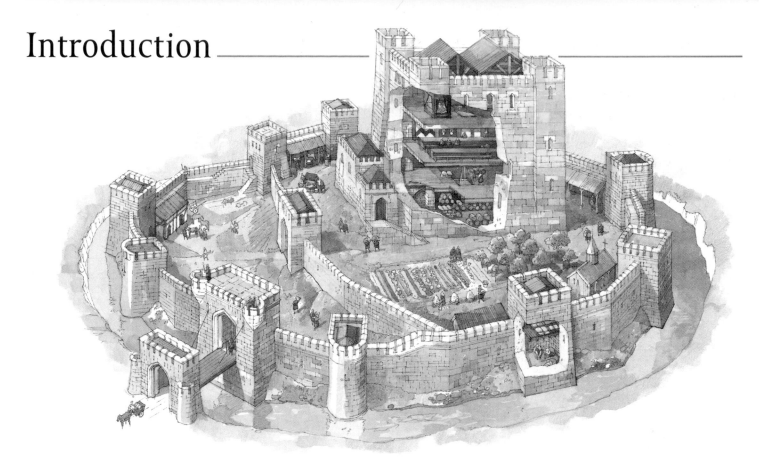

The medieval period is the name given to 1,000 years of history, from about 500 to about 1500 in the Christian calendar. They begin with the fall of the last of the great civilisations of the Mediterranean region, and last up to the beginning of the Modern Age.

During that time, the centres of civilisation were the same as they had been in the ancient world. Most of them had only small contacts with each other, and some had no contact at all (before 1492 Europeans did not know that America existed). All these civilisations had their ups and downs, and some of them greatly increased their own lands by wars of conquest. But none of them ever held power over the others.

One effect of what we call civilisation is that changes happen faster, and although changes came much more slowly in the medieval period than they do now, nowhere did everything remain the same for 1,000 years. China was in many ways the most advanced civilisation. It became a single empire and enjoyed a 'golden age' under the powerful Tang dynasty, and again under the Sung. Japan also

became an empire in the 7th century, though a much smaller one. India enjoyed its golden age under the Gupta Empire. In Europe, the idea of one great power, like the Roman Empire that had dominated the ancient world, still lived on in people's minds, and the idea of unity was helped by the power of the Church under the rule of the Pope. But by 1500 many of the nations that make up modern Europe had already appeared.

One cause of disaster to the centres of civilisation was attack by nomadic peoples from central Asia. The Huns, for example, destroyed the Gupta Empire in the 6th century. The last of these conquerors were the Mongols in the 13th century. They created the biggest empire the world had yet seen, although it did not last long.

A greater disturbance to the balance of the old civilisations was the rise of Islam. Beginning among a small group of Arabs, Islam spread throughout much of Asia, North Africa and large parts of Europe and West Africa between the 7th and 15th centuries. The clash of two aggressive religions – Christianity and Islam – could be heard throughout the medieval period.

The Arabs and Islam

In the 7th century a new power appeared in the Middle East – the Arabs. They were inspired by the teachings of the Prophet Muhammad, and conquered an empire larger than the Roman Empire.

Muhammad and Islam

Muhammad was born in the 6th century in Arabia. Arabia was mostly desert, with many small towns built beside oases. Muhammad grew up in Mecca, which was a great trading city. Muhammad believed he was inspired by God to create a new religion. His message was this: there is only one God (Allah), and Muhammad is his prophet. Muhammad's teachings annoyed Mecca's wealthy merchants. He and his followers were attacked, and Muhammad was forbidden to preach. So in 622 they moved to the rival city of Medina. This journey is called the Hejira. It marks the beginning of Islam. In the Muslim calendar it is year 1.

Islam is not just a religion, it is a whole way of life, with people united by their faith in Allah. The followers of Islam are called Muslims. The teachings of Muhammad are recorded in the Koran, the holy book of Islam. After Muhammad's death (632), the Arabs set out to conquer the Middle East and North Africa for Islam. Many peoples, including the Christians of Egypt and Syria, welcomed Arab rule, which was not harsh. People of different religions were not usually persecuted.

◁ This is the courtyard of the great mosque at Damascus in Syria, first built in 705-715. Muslims soon developed their own type of religious building, with a dome, minaret (a tower for calling people to prayer) and a large space inside for prayer.

The spread of Islam

The leader of Islam was called the caliph. He was a ruler as well as a religious leader. There were quarrels about who should be caliph, and in 656 the third caliph was murdered. Islam then split into two branches, Sunni and Shi'a. After a civil war, the Umayyads in Syria took control. They ruled from Damascus for nearly 100 years.

The Abbasid family, with Shi'ite support, overthrew the Umayyads in 750. They shifted the centre of Islam from Syria to Iraq, and moved the capital to Baghdad. Islam was no longer an Arab empire. Other peoples, especially Persians, played leading parts. The army became a force of trained slaves, called Mamelukes. The caliphs grew more powerful. There were roughly four classes of people in Islam. At the top were Arab Muslims, followed by non-Arab Muslims, then people of other religions and, at the bottom, slaves.

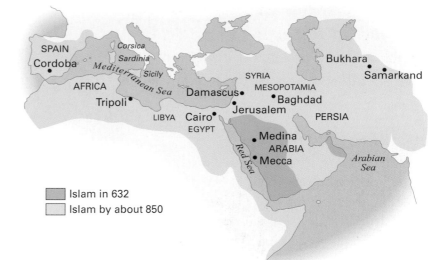

Islam in 632
Islam by about 850

The golden age of Islam

Under the caliphs, a brilliant new civilisation developed. With its libraries and observatories, Islam was superior in knowledge to Christian Europe. Its scholars studied the learning of ancient Greece, as well as Egypt, the Middle East and Asia. It was also better governed, and less intolerant. Every Muslim who could afford it had to go on a pilgrimage to Mecca, and merchants travelled to India and China to buy luxuries. On these journeys they learned more about the world. Islam also produced fine new styles in art and architecture.

△ Although Islam grew by conquest, many peoples welcomed it.

▷ Islamic scholars wrote beautiful books by hand and artists illustrated them with intricate miniature paintings. Islamic art was a mixture of Arab, Turkish and Persian traditions.

Court life

Some of the stories of the 'Arabian Nights' are set in the court of Harun ar-Rashid. At his court could be seen the most amazing riches, like this silver bowl (below), and the finest musicians, artists and scholars in the world. Islamic craftsmen invented a brilliantly painted new form of pottery, called 'lustreware'.

The last caliph

After the death of the Abbasid caliph Harun ar-Rashid (809), the empire began to break down. By the 10th century the caliphs had little power. A branch of the Umayyad family set up their own caliph in Spain. The Shi'ite Ismailis conquered Egypt and built Cairo. The Seljuk Turks captured Baghdad in 1055. The last Abbasid caliph was thrown out by the Mongols in 1258.

The Rise of the Chinese Empire

Under the early Tang emperors, the Chinese Empire grew larger and richer than it had been under the Han. Although Tang rule ended in chaos, Chinese civilisation flourished again during the Song dynasty.

The Tang dynasty

After many years of civil war and foreign rule, China was reunited by the Sui emperors (581-618), followed by the Tang (618-906). The Tang dynasty was the most successful in ancient China. The emperor was called the 'Son of Heaven'. He strengthened his control by using loyal, trained officials to run the central government, rather than untrustworthy nobles. Tang emperors had the Great Wall repaired, and enlarged the empire far into central Asia, until they were stopped by the Arabs in 751. There was one female Tang ruler, the Empress Wu.

▽ This beautiful horse with a polo player shows the skill of Tang artists. It is made of porcelain. The Chinese loved horses, and had figures like this buried with them. As early as the 1st century BC, Chinese emperors sent expeditions to buy horses from breeders in central Asia.

The Tang capital, Ch'ang-an, was the world's largest city. There you might see monks from Tibet, merchants from Arabia, and travellers from the Middle East, Korea and Japan. The population of China grew. According to a census it was over 50 million by 754. Country people were better off than they had been before, although landlords held complete power over the peasants. A series of rebellions by the peasants eventually destroyed the Tang dynasty, and China split into many small kingdoms.

◁ This busy street in a Chinese city was drawn in about 1100. Chinese cities were large. Over a million people lived in Hangzhou. It took 200 tonnes of rice a day to feed them all.

The Silk Road

Chinese craftsmen produced beautiful goods, such as silk fabric, which people wanted to buy. As a result, trade developed between China and other countries. From the 3rd century BC to the 15th century AD, China was linked to the west by the Old Silk Road. This long and dangerous road stretched from the Great Wall to Iran. It passed along the edge of the Takla Makan Desert, 1,000 km of nothing but sand, then crossed the Tian Shan mountain range. One branch went south, over the high Pamir Mountains into India. Traders from many countries met along the Road.

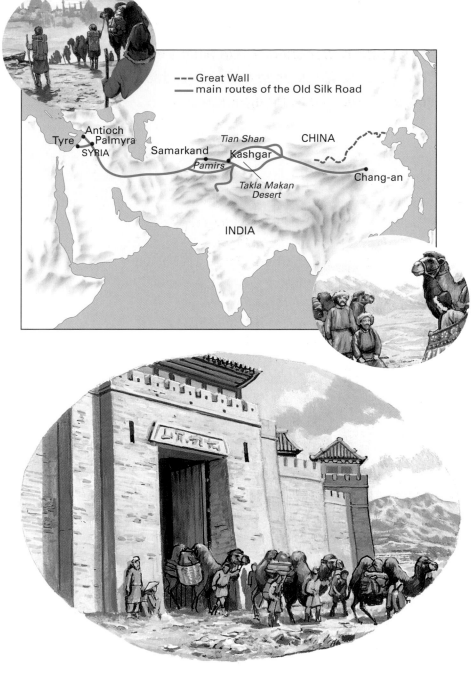

Buddhism

Buddhism became very popular in China during the hard times before the Sui reunited the country. Buddhists built tens of thousands of temples and monasteries. Buddhism was so popular that it threatened the old religions of Confucianism and Taoism, and even the power of the emperor. In 845 the Emperor Wu Zong closed many temples and monasteries. This harsh treatment soon stopped, as Buddhism no longer threatened the emperor's rule.

The Song dynasty

Fifty years after the end of the Tang dynasty, the Song reunited the small kingdoms of China. This was a wonderful age for poetry, arts and learning. The blue-and-white pottery which later became popular in Europe, was just one new development. Among the others were landscape painting and calligraphy (the art of writing with an ink brush). Chinese knowledge of science was also advanced: books were printed, and engineering and medicine were taught in government schools. Water-powered machines were used in industry, and two crops of rice each year kept the Chinese well fed.

Although it had gunpowder, Song China (960-1279) was not a great military power. The empire was far smaller than under the Tang. After 1127 the Song lost control of the north, and in 1279 China was conquered by the Mongols.

△ Goods passed along the Silk Road from China to Central Asia. From there, they went to the Mediterranean and, in the end, reached European markets. On the way they were bought and sold several times. Above, a gate in the Great Wall, and scenes of caravan travel.

The Rulers of Japan

The Japanese were never invaded, for they lived on islands, protected by the sea. Although the Japanese learned many of their customs from China, their civilisation was very different.

▷ The mountains made it difficult for the central government to control Japan's warrior clans. Farming land was scarce but fertile. The Japanese relied on their large rice crops and on fishing for food.

▽ The Kamakura Buddha is over 13 metres high, and made of bronze. Buddhism, especially the form called Zen, was a powerful influence on Japanese civilisation.

Emperors and shoguns

Japan has had a monarchy for longer than any other country. The first emperor of Japan lived over 2,000 years ago. However, a system of central government began only under Prince Shotoku Taishi (572-622), based on the system in Tang China. At this time most Japanese lived in the southern islands. Another people, the Ainu, lived in the north. Their descendants still do.

Shotoku made Nara the capital. He also encouraged Buddhism, which became a great influence on Japanese civilisation, though it never destroyed the older religion, Shinto. In 794, the Emperor Kammu moved the government to Heian (Kyoto), to get away from the Buddhists in Nara. But there it fell under the influence of powerful clans. For many centuries these mighty families provided the real rulers of Japan, the 'shoguns'. Shoguns were military rulers. The emperor was supposed to be a god, but in reality he had very little power over his people.

Japanese arts

The nobles had plenty of leisure time, which they used to practise and enjoy the arts. They wrote poetry in beautiful script, which they learned from the Chinese, and illustrated it with delicate landscape painting. Under Buddhist influence, the Japanese made art forms out of such activities as paper folding (origami) and gardening. Gardens made from rocks and pebbles, with no plants, were designed as a picture to be seen from the house. Japan's special form of theatre was the Noh drama. Noh plays were like ceremonies, with dancing and chanting. Actors wore masks, and there was no scenery.

△ A Kabuki play. Theatre was one of the liveliest Japanese arts. Besides the Noh drama, more popular plays developed in the towns in the 17th century. Kabuki was one form. Bunraku was another, involving puppets.

Japanese and Europeans

Europeans first visited Japan in 1543. By then the Ashikaga shogunate had collapsed, and Japan was ruled by local lords, called 'daimyo'. The daimyo were amazed by European technology, especially guns which they were eager to buy. European missionaries converted many people to Christianity. Soon after this, Japan was reunited by three great daimyo. One of them, Tokugawa Iyeasu, set himself up as a shogun in 1603 and ruled all Japan. He distrusted all foreign ideas, drove out the Europeans and even killed many Japanese Christians, after they rebelled against him.

The samurai

'Samurai' means a servant. A samurai was a warrior. Like a knight in Europe, he fought for his local lord. His life was controlled by a strict code of behaviour, called 'bushido', which was influenced by Zen Buddhism. Honour, loyalty and courage were the great samurai virtues. A samurai preferred death in battle to surrender. A samurai who lost his honour would kill himself with his own sword. Under the Tokugawa, samurai became officials and governors, as well as warriors, but their code of behaviour lived on.

Mauryan and Gupta India

India is protected by sea and the Himalayan Mountains. Invaders could reach it only from the north-west. Over the centuries, many conquerors entered by that route and won empires in northern India.

The Mauryan Empire

Soon after Alexander's invasion of India in 327 BC, Chandragupta Maurya became king of Magadha, a large kingdom in the valley of the Ganges. He made it the centre of a huge empire. Under Mauryan rule, farmers and villagers lived well. Trade grew because good roads were built, including the main highway of northern India, later called the Grand Trunk Road. Mauryan government was well-organised. A good system for collecting taxes meant that the emperor did not have to make war to gain treasure. The greatest Mauryan ruler was Asoka (273-232 BC), Chandragupta's grandson. He was a great warrior, but he grew tired of killing, and became a peace-loving Buddhist. Along the roads Asoka planted banyan trees to give shade, and stone pillars, beautifully decorated and inscribed with his laws and messages of goodwill and justice.

▷ Empires in ancient India covered a different area from the modern state. Asoka's empire stretched from Afghanistan to the Bay of Bengal.

⬭ Mauryan Empire in about 232 BC
▢ Gupta Empire in about 410
— Mauryan highway

▽ A farming village in Gupta times. Carts like this were used by the Indus Valley people 4,000 years ago. They are still used today.

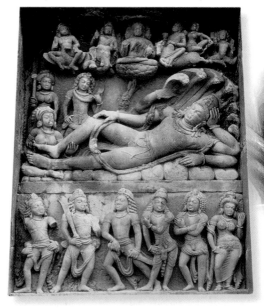

△ This sculpture from a Hindu temple shows the god Vishnu sleeping on the serpent-god Ananta.

The Gupta Empire

After Asoka, the Mauryan Empire broke up into smaller states. A new empire was created by the Guptas in the 4th-6th centuries AD. This was the 'golden age' of Indian civilisation. Magnificent temples were built. Dancing and music flourished, and sculpture and painting were at their best. Great literature was written in Sanskrit, the ancient Indian language. Mathematicians used algebra and invented the decimal system. They first had the idea of a number 0, or zero. Hinduism influenced a new form of Buddhism, called Mahayana. It was less strict and more open to new ideas. Although the Gupta Empire was destroyed by the Huns in the 6th century, the Gupta civilisation lived on in India.

Castes

The Hindu caste system was based on religious beliefs. Hindus believed that when the world was created, everyone was divided into four classes. The Brahmin were priests and scholars, the Khatriya were warriors and princes, the Vaishya were craftsmen and merchants (like the man weighing his goods, above), and the Sudra were the labourers. The caste system began in Mauryan times, and later many more castes developed. The poorest people had no caste. They were the 'untouchables'. It was almost impossible for a person to change his caste, or marry someone of another caste. This kept people in their place, but it also gave them a sense of belonging.

The Muslims in India

Arabs had traded with eastern Indian states for centuries. They built mosques there in the 9th century. Much later, Islam reached north India from central Asia. An Afghan conqueror, Muhammad of Ghor, made himself sultan of Delhi in about 1200. The Delhi sultans were the greatest power in India for the next 200 years, but this was not a true empire. It was made up of independent states which paid taxes to the rulers in Delhi. Muslim rule almost ended Buddhism in India, but Muslims and Hindus lived together, although not always peacefully. The Delhi of the sultans was destroyed by the Mongols, who captured the city in 1398.

Southern India

Once, most of India was occupied by people sometimes called 'Dravidians'. The invaders of northern India pushed many of them south. Here they formed independent kingdoms, such as the Tamil states in the far south, and the Cheras in Kerala. These Hindu kingdoms often fought each other. Many Indian ideas and customs spread from south India to Sri Lanka, Myanmar (Burma) and south-east Asia.

Medieval Africa

Africa was a continent of villages, towns and small kingdoms. Many people lived around the coasts and in the Sahel, the region south of the Sahara Desert and north of the tropical forest. In West Africa, large empires rose and fell, while rich city states developed along the east coast.

West African empires

Most African peoples south of the Sahara were farmers and cattle herders. A wide variety of crops was grown, and new crops from Asia and elsewhere spread quickly through the continent. Cattle and other animals were kept in many different regions and climates.

Most African kingdoms were small. However, several African kingdoms became so powerful that they conquered their neighbours and created large empires. In West Africa there were three different empires, but they did not exist at the same time. When one kingdom grew weak, another one took over. The first West African empire was called Ghana. Its power was greatest in about the 10th century.

Attacks by Muslims from the north ruined Ghana. In the 13th century it was replaced by the larger empire of Mali. Because Mali's rulers were Muslims themselves and had a strong army, the danger from northern Muslims ended. Visitors reported that Mali was rich and peaceful, with little crime, but in the 15th century it too was conquered. The new empire belonged to the Songhay, former subjects of Mali, from Gao on the Niger. Theirs was the largest African empire yet.

▷ African states had no clear borders, and government control grew weaker far from their centres. The three great West African empires existed at different times. Another large empire, Kanem-Borno, lay to the east of Songhay. The ports on the east coast had Muslim rulers, and grew rich on trade with Arabia and the Middle East.

◁ Sculpture was the finest of the African arts. The bronze heads from Benin (Nigeria) are especially famous. This one was made in the 16th century.

Map labels: Fez, MOROCCO, Tripoli, Alexandria, EGYPT, Mecca, SAHARA, Nile, Timbuktu, Gao, Jenne, SAHEL, Niger, ABYSSINIA, Benin City, BENIN, Congo, Zambezi, Great Zimbabwe, Sofala

Legend:
- Ghana
- Mali
- Songhay
- Kanem-Borno
- Karanga
- trade routes

Trade across the Sahara

The riches of the West African rulers came from gold. When Sultan Musa of Mali made the pilgrimage to Mecca, he took 1.5 tonnes of gold for travel expenses! Gold was traded for salt from the Sahara salt pans. Salt was very difficult to get so it cost as much as gold. Merchants from North Africa brought cloth, horses and iron weapons across the Sahara in exchange for gold and slaves, which they sold in the Mediterranean region. Even European kings who had never heard of Africa had coins made from West African gold. Most Africans used other objects, such as cowrie shells or pieces of iron, as money.

◁ This extraordinary church was carved out of solid rock by early Christians at Lalibela in Abyssinia (modern Ethiopia) before 1000. Abyssinia became a Christian country as early as the 4th century, when missionaries from Syria converted the king to Christianity. The country remained an independent, Christian kingdom until the 20th century.

▽ Many people crossed the Sahara in ancient times. Traders joined together in large groups called caravans, with hundreds of camels carrying their goods. They travelled in caravans to protect them from attack by the blue-veiled Tuareg, the roving nomads of the desert.

Great Zimbabwe

These stone buildings, built 700 years ago, are the ruins of Great Zimbabwe in what is now modern Zimbabwe. The outer wall was built of granite blocks. It was 250 metres long and up to 10 metres high. When it was built Great Zimbabwe was the centre of the Karanga trading empire. As in West Africa, gold was the reason for its wealth. The gold was mined by women in mines deep in the forest. After it was refined, the gold was carried down to the coast and shipped to trading ports such as Sofala.

The Birth of European Nations

Between the 5th and 10th centuries, European tribes formed Christian kingdoms ruled by warrior kings. The most successful were the Franks. Their king Charlemagne created an empire that was the foundation for some of the nations of Europe today.

land inherited by Charlemagne in 771

additional land gained by Charlemagne by 814

Charlemagne and the Pope

Charlemagne united the Franks under his rule in 771, and increased his empire by wars of conquest. He was a skilful ruler as well as a great conqueror. He forced the people he conquered to become Christians. His court at Aachen became the centre of learning and art in Europe. The greatest authority in medieval Europe was the Church, headed by the Pope in Rome. The Church expected everyone to follow its teaching. It owned a lot of land, and the Pope had great authority, but he had no army. He needed an ally, a powerful ruler who would support the Church, with force if necessary. The Pope found that ally in Charlemagne.

On Christmas Day 800, the Pope crowned Charlemagne Emperor in Rome. He became a ruler like the old Roman emperors, although his was a Christian empire.

△ Charlemagne fought Lombards in Italy, Saxons in Germany, Muslims in Spain, and many others.

▷ The finest buildings in Europe were the monasteries that followed the rule of St Benedict (480-547). The largest was at Cluny, in France. Only one tower of the old building survives.

◁ The first great revival of European art since Roman times took place under the Frankish kings (called Carolingians). This ivory sculpture was made as part of a book cover, in about 800.

After Charlemagne

After Charlemagne died (814), his empire was split up among his descendants. The two biggest parts later became the nations of France and Germany. The idea of a Christian empire lived on. In the 10th century the German king, Otto I, was crowned by the Pope. He took the title Holy (meaning 'Christian') Roman Emperor, though he controlled only what is now Germany and Italy. The title was held by German kings for nearly 1,000 years.

The Anglo-Saxons

In the 5th and 6th centuries Angles, Saxons and other tribes from northern Germany invaded England. They formed several small kingdoms and became Christians. In the 9th century, the Vikings overran all these kingdoms except one, Wessex. The King of Wessex, Alfred the Great, defended the south of England successfully. After his death (899), the whole of England (though not Scotland, Wales or Ireland) was united under the kings who came after him.

△ Alfred was England's Charlemagne. He encouraged education and learning, and created a system of law. This jewel portrait probably belonged to him. He may have lost it in marshes while dodging the Vikings.

The Church

Priests were part of everyday life in Christian Europe, from royal court to poor village. The parish priest was often the only person in the village who could read. His sermons were the only source of news and information.

Monasteries were great centres of Christian civilisation. As well as praying, monks farmed the land and cared for the sick (there were no other hospitals). Some were teachers and scholars. The only records of these times were written by monks. Bede wrote the first history of the English in 731.

Women could not be priests, but they could become nuns in their own religious houses. A nun could rise to be an abbess, a powerful person in the district. Well-born women without a husband often became nuns.

Some of the finest examples of Carolingian art were illustrated copies of religious books. One monk might spend many years working on a single book. The illustration above shows the Pope consecrating the Abbey of Cluny in 1095.

The Vikings

In the 8th-10th centuries, bands of people from Scandinavia left their homes to search for land and wealth. We call them Vikings. Some of them were robbers, but others were traders or colonists.

Raiders

The Vikings came from Denmark, Norway and Sweden. They were a farming people but, because they lived close to the sea, they were also skilful sailors. They may have decided to leave their homes because good farming land was scarce. The Vikings first attacked northern Europe as raiders. As fierce fighters and non-Christians, they terrified peaceful people, killing some and capturing others to sell as slaves. They often attacked monasteries, which were not well-protected, and carried off valuable objects such as gold crosses. Other Vikings sailed up rivers to attack inland cities. In 845, 100 ships sailed up the Seine to Paris. The king gave them 3,000 kg of silver to go away.

▷ The Vikings had a form of writing made up of signs, or letters, called runes. The families of famous people made rune stones like this one to describe their deeds. This one in Sweden was written in memory of a dead son.

◁ Viking longships were the finest ships in Europe. They were light but strong, made of oak or pinewood, and could bend a little, which allowed them to survive the rough northern seas. They were mainly powered by oars, but also had a sail and could go as fast as 10 knots (20 kph). Longships were warships, and perfect for surprise attacks. They could sail in shallow water and land on a beach.

Traders and travellers

Viking merchants from Sweden crossed the Baltic Sea to Russia in the 9th century. They set up trading posts there among the Slav tribes. They played some part in creating Novgorod and the first Russian state. Some Swedish merchants travelled by boat, down Russian rivers to the Black Sea and the Caspian. Riding camels, they travelled to Constantinople, where some found work and settled. Many Swedes joined the Byzantine emperor's personal guard. Other Swedish merchants travelled as far as Baghdad in Persia.

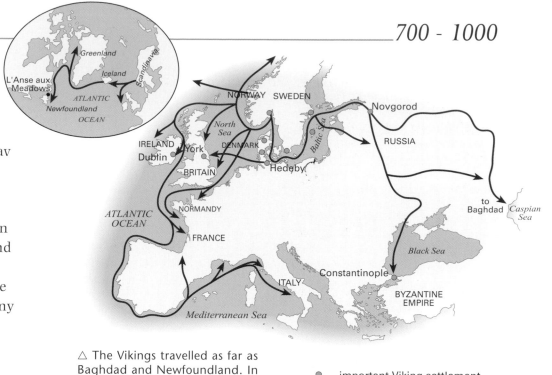

△ The Vikings travelled as far as Baghdad and Newfoundland. In Iceland, the Norwegians founded a new European nation. At first it was governed by an assembly of chiefs, Europe's first 'parliament'.

● important Viking settlement
→ Viking routes

Settlers

After the early raids on northern Europe, the Vikings left Scandinavia in larger numbers. They were looking for land where they could live, farm and trade. They conquered half of England, and almost destroyed the Celtic civilisation of Ireland, founding new kingdoms in York, Dublin and other places. The French king gave Normandy to a large group of Vikings, who promised to defend his kingdom against other Vikings. The descendants of this group were the Normans, who became a great power in Europe in the 11th century.

Vikings from Norway sailed far into the Atlantic. They found lands where no one lived, and settled in the Faroe Islands and Iceland. From here, they explored further west and settled in Greenland. They even sailed to North America, but did not settle there because the local people drove them off.

Everyday life

In most of Scandinavia, the Vikings built houses of wood. In Iceland and Greenland, which had few trees, they used stone and chunks of turf. Houses had no chimney nor windows, just a door. Inside was one large room where people lived and worked and children played games (until told to play outside). Sometimes they slept here too, on the raised parts at the sides of the room. Women cooked on an open fire, and a hole in the roof let out the smoke.

Lords and Priests in Europe

*In the 11th to 15th centuries, most ordinary people in Europe,
as in other continents, made their living from farming.
Their lives were ruled by the lord who owned the land,
and by the teaching of the Church.*

Feudalism

After the Vikings, there were no more great
invasions in Europe. The continent settled down
into kingdoms. The king was the 'owner' of his
kingdom, and gave land to the nobles in exchange
for their support, especially in war. The nobles in
turn gave land to lesser lords in exchange for
their service.

We call this system 'feudalism', the arrangement
of people promising loyalty and service in return
for land and protection. Not everyone obeyed
these arrangements. There was plenty of fighting
between nobles, and nobles sometimes rebelled
against their king.

The Normans were the most successful feudal
power in the 11th century. They fought all
over Europe and in 1066 they invaded England
and defeated the English king at the battle
of Hastings. Their leader, William the
Conqueror, set up a strong feudal system,
supported by the powerful castles of
his lords.

The Church and the king

The greatest authority in Europe was the Church,
which was ruled by the Pope. Kings and lords ruled
people's bodies, but the Church ruled their souls.
People feared that if they disobeyed Church
teaching, they would go to hell when they died.

The Church was rich and powerful. Kings and
nobles promised to support the Church, but kings
did not like sharing their power. The division of
power between the Church and the King caused
problems. Bishops were powerful lords as well as
priests. But should they obey the King, or the
Pope? This question caused many quarrels,
especially between the Pope and the Holy Roman
Emperor. In England, Archbishop Thomas Becket
and King Henry II argued about the rights of
priests, and this led to Becket's murder in 1170.

▽ In the 12th century, stone castles
were built all over Europe. They
usually followed a simple plan. A
large central building, called the
keep, stood in a bailey or
courtyard, protected by walls
and towers. This castle has
two baileys and a moat,
for extra protection.

▽ The loudest sound in the countryside in the Middle Ages was the sound of church bells. The church was the centre of village life.

Everyone was supposed to go to services, but only the priest understood them, as they were in Latin. Only priests and travelling friars knew about events outside the village.

The Crusades

In 1096, the Pope appealed to Christian rulers to reconquer Jerusalem, which had been captured by the Seljuk Turks. The result was a long series of holy wars, called crusades, against the Muslims in Palestine. The First Crusade captured Jerusalem, and founded several small Christian kingdoms in the Middle East. However the Muslims fought back, and Christians gradually lost interest in crusading. By 1300 almost all the Holy Land was back in Muslim hands.

Crusades were also fought against the Muslims in Spain. These were more successful. By 1492, the last Muslim state in Spain had fallen.

Pilgrimage

Christians, like Muslims, made long journeys to holy places. This was called going on pilgrimage. All kinds of people became pilgrims. For some it was a kind of holiday. One of the most popular sites in Europe was Santiago de Compostella in Spain, where an apostle of Jesus was said to be buried. In England, pilgrims flocked to the shrine of Archbishop Becket in Canterbury. The holiest place was Jerusalem, but it was far away, and when the Turks captured the city, people could not visit it.

▽ This 15th-century painting shows how later French artists imagined scenes of the Crusades. It shows the Muslim leader Saladin recapturing Jerusalem in 1187.

Everyday Life in Medieval Europe

Life in Europe between 1000 and 1500 was difficult. Most people were poor, they had to work hard, and they died young. But even poor people were able to enjoy themselves a few times during the year.

The life of peasants

Nobles, priests and monks made up only about a tenth of the population. The rest were peasants. Most peasants in the countryside lived as 'serfs' in villages or manors, which were owned by a lord (one lord might own many villages). Serfs worked on their lord's farm, and were allowed some land of their own in return. Although they were not slaves, serfs had few rights. They could not marry or leave their village without the lord's permission. The lord even had his own law court where he punished criminals and settled arguments.

Medieval homes and food

Most houses were built of timber, or sticks and mud. Few people could afford bricks or stone. Peasants' homes had few rooms, and the people often shared the space with farm animals. Even at the end of the 15th century, only the rich had glass windows or chimneys. Women usually cooked on an open fire, and a hole in the roof let out the smoke. Houses often caught fire.

Rich people ate meat every day, but for the peasants it was a luxury. They ate mostly porridge, some cheese, and thick vegetable soup. They grew their own grain and vegetables on the land their lord allowed them, as well as working on his land. They made their bread at home and baked it in the village oven. When times were hard, they made flour from acorns and soup from nettles.

△ A village's mill belonged to the lord. It ground all the people's grain, but they had to pay the miller.

▽ This picture shows peasants working on the harvest with the lord's representative watching over them. They are cutting the wheat with scythes.

Women and children

A woman from a good family could either marry or become a nun. If she married, her father chose her husband. Upper class marriage was a business, in which a contract was made between the husband and his wife's father. Wives were supposed to be obedient to their husbands (but sometimes the wife made the decisions). Poorer women worked in the fields and, more often, at home, looking after their children, preparing food, and making clothes.

Mothers often died when they had a baby, and families were lucky if one child in four survived. Children worked from an early age. Boys who were going to be knights or craftsmen began training at the age of eight. They went to live with the man who taught them. Girls learned from their mothers. Few peasant children went to school or could read. Schools were run by the Church, mainly to train priests or monks. As times changed, more boys – and a few girls – of noble families went to school.

The Black Death

The Black Death was an epidemic (large-scale outbreak) of plague, a disease carried by fleas on rats. It started in Asia in 1347, and spread across Europe in 1348-49. It was the greatest disaster Europe had ever suffered. In three years, nearly one-third of the population died. Many people believed that it was a punishment from God.

◁ The black figure with the scythe is Death. He stands on a plague victim.

Entertainment

Peasants rested on Sundays and on other holy days. They would visit feasts and fairs, where jugglers and singers performed, and useful services were available, such as pulling teeth. Boys and men practised archery, and played a rough form of football. Life was cruel, and people enjoyed cock-fighting and bear-baiting.

▽ A popular entertainment among medieval nobles was the joust or tournament. Knights competed against each other on horseback.

European Towns

In the 12th and 13th centuries more goods were produced, trade was increasing fast, and the old feudal arrangements were breaking down. The merchants who traded across Europe and even further became more important.

Caring for the sick

A doctor tries to find out what is wrong with his patient by examining his urine. The sick man must have been rich, as doctors were expensive. Their cures seldom worked because they did not know the causes of disease. Monks or nuns ran hospitals in some towns.

The rise of the merchants

In 1300 only a small number of people lived in towns. However, important changes were taking place there. Some merchants, bankers and skilled craftsmen, such as goldsmiths, were becoming richer than the lord who ruled the town. All over western Europe, craftsmen and merchants formed groups called guilds to protect their trade. They often managed to make their town independent of the local lord. In Italy and Germany especially, large towns were ruled by rich merchants, not by nobles. The richest place in Europe was probably Venice, in Italy. That city's wealth was based on trade with the East.

△ This beautiful Italian angel is a reliquary. Reliquaries were made to hold a 'relic', such as a bone from a dead saint. Pilgrims often travelled long distances to pray near a holy relic.

△ The difference between the country and the towns was less great than in later times. Even townspeople kept chickens and a pig, and grew vegetables, while in the country people made their own clothes and tools. In every town and village, the largest building was the church. The great cathedrals were the finest creations of all Christian art.

The growth of trade

The growth of trade was helped by the development of banking in the 14th century. Merchants were able to buy and sell on credit. Silk and other luxuries arrived from the East, but the largest trade was in wool and woollen cloth. The leading traders in northern Europe were in the Hanseatic League, a group of 150 north German towns, led by Hamburg and Lübeck, which traded with each other. They also had special trade agreements in cities such as London in England, Bruges in Flanders and Bergen in Norway.

Trading cities were by the sea or on major rivers, because goods were usually carried by ships. Even though ships were often wrecked, water transport was safer and quicker than using the roads.

The end of feudal life

As a result of war, famine and disease, the population of Europe decreased in the 14th century. This was a time of changes, and of problems. Wars and rebellions became more common. Even peasants rebelled against their lords. The old feudal arrangements were disappearing, and money was becoming more important. By the 15th century, most peasants were no longer serfs. They paid the lord rent for their land, and he paid them cash for their work. Kings paid professional soldiers to fight for them, instead of asking nobles to lead their peasants into battle.

The Mongols

The Mongols were the last of the nomadic, horse-riding peoples from central Asia who invaded the towns and farms of Asia and Europe. Under Genghis Khan, they conquered lands stretching from China to eastern Europe. It was the largest empire the world had seen, though it did not last long.

▽ The Mongols lived in large tents, called yurts. They were made of felt on a light wooden frame, and could be put up in less than an hour.

Warrior herdsmen

The Mongol tribes moved around the plain of east-central Asia with their herds of sheep, goats and cattle. The leader of one tribe, Genghis Khan, united them in about 1206. He dreamed of ruling the world, and under his leadership the Mongols conquered a large empire with amazing speed. The Mongols were swift and skilful horsemen, and planned their attacks carefully. Mongol leaders (called khans) would never start a battle without first carefully investigating the enemy's position, and then deciding on the best way to attack.

▽ A fierce battle between Mongol tribes. Until they were united by Genghis Khan, the different tribes sometimes fought each other. Mongols were excellent horsemen. Each man owned four or five horses, captured from the wild Mongolian herds. Often a man's best horse was buried with him. A warrior carried several throwing spears and a curved sword, but his best weapon was his bow. He could hit a target 300 metres away.

Marco Polo

The Mongol conquest reopened the old trade routes from Europe to the East. Adventurous Italian traders followed the Old Silk Road to China. One of these was a young man called Marco Polo. He met the Mongol emperor Kublai Khan in 1275 (shown in the painting below, where Marco Polo receives the emperor's golden seal). The emperor seems to have hired him as a government official. Marco Polo's Asian travels lasted 24 years, and when he returned to Italy he told his story to someone who wrote a book about them. These tales of a great, strange civilisation in the East astonished Europe. Some people thought the story was made up. Marco Polo certainly exaggerated, but we now know that many of the things that people doubted were true.

Mongol China

The Mongol conquest was a savage blow to Chinese civilisation, and caused dreadful destruction. Genghis Khan's grandson, Kublai Khan, became the first emperor of the Mongol dynasty in China (also called the Yuan dynasty). Kublai Khan was a wise and intelligent ruler. He kept Chinese customs, supported Buddhism, and improved trade. But he never trusted Chinese officials. He tried to spread his empire further and invade Japan, but the invasion was ruined by storms which sank his ships.

▽ The Mongol Empire at its largest. The Mongol invasions in Asia and Europe had surprisingly few lasting effects. Not even the language has survived anywhere outside Mongolia.

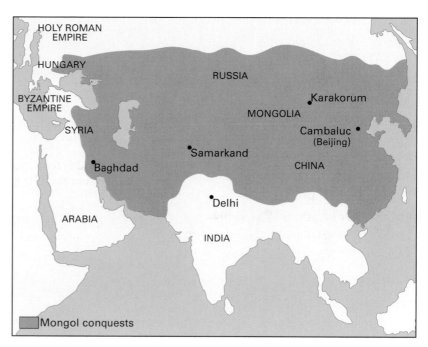

The end of the Mongol empire

After the death of Genghis Khan (1227), the Mongol empire was divided between his four sons. His son, Ogudai, became the Great Khan. The Mongols went on to invade Russia and Hungary, and might have conquered all Europe, but Ogudai died in 1241, and his brothers argued over who should replace him. The conquest of China was completed by Kublai Khan. The Great Khan's brother, Hülegü, invaded west Asia. He captured Baghdad and killed the caliph. But in 1260 a large Mameluke army defeated the Mongols in Palestine. That was the end of Mongol conquest. By 1300 the empire had broken up and was ruled by four separate khans.

Tamerlane

Mongol conquest was started again by Timur, or Tamerlane, in 1380-1405. Timur may have been a descendant of Genghis Khan. Like Genghis, he was a great war leader, and just as cruel. But he had no ability as a governor and did not create an empire. He conquered western Asia and destroyed the Khanate of the Golden Horde, which was ruled by one of Genghis Khan's descendants. He invaded India, and died while trying to conquer China.

The Medieval World

Over a thousand years separated the ancient world from the beginning of modern times. In that period new civilisations arose. The most powerful were based on religion: Christianity in Europe, and Islam, centred on the Middle East. In other regions, such as

	600-749	750-899	900-1049

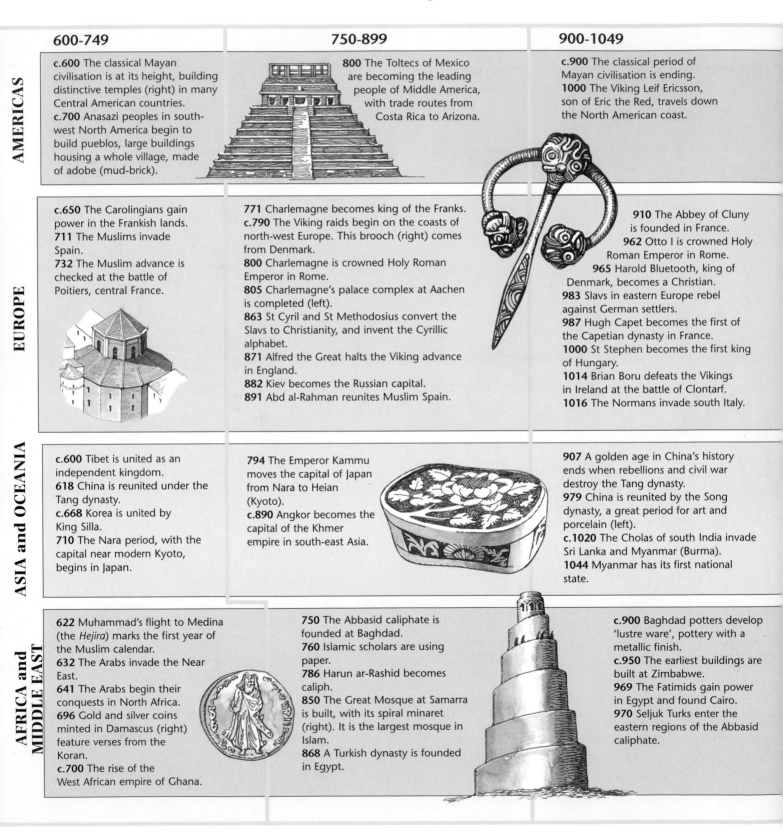

AMERICAS

c.600 The classical Mayan civilisation is at its height, building distinctive temples (right) in many Central American countries.
c.700 Anasazi peoples in south-west North America begin to build pueblos, large buildings housing a whole village, made of adobe (mud-brick).

800 The Toltecs of Mexico are becoming the leading people of Middle America, with trade routes from Costa Rica to Arizona.

c.900 The classical period of Mayan civilisation is ending.
1000 The Viking Leif Ericsson, son of Eric the Red, travels down the North American coast.

EUROPE

c.650 The Carolingians gain power in the Frankish lands.
711 The Muslims invade Spain.
732 The Muslim advance is checked at the battle of Poitiers, central France.

771 Charlemagne becomes king of the Franks.
c.790 The Viking raids begin on the coasts of north-west Europe. This brooch (right) comes from Denmark.
800 Charlemagne is crowned Holy Roman Emperor in Rome.
805 Charlemagne's palace complex at Aachen is completed (left).
863 St Cyril and St Methodosius convert the Slavs to Christianity, and invent the Cyrillic alphabet.
871 Alfred the Great halts the Viking advance in England.
882 Kiev becomes the Russian capital.
891 Abd al-Rahman reunites Muslim Spain.

910 The Abbey of Cluny is founded in France.
962 Otto I is crowned Holy Roman Emperor in Rome.
965 Harold Bluetooth, king of Denmark, becomes a Christian.
983 Slavs in eastern Europe rebel against German settlers.
987 Hugh Capet becomes the first of the Capetian dynasty in France.
1000 St Stephen becomes the first king of Hungary.
1014 Brian Boru defeats the Vikings in Ireland at the battle of Clontarf.
1016 The Normans invade south Italy.

ASIA and OCEANIA

c.600 Tibet is united as an independent kingdom.
618 China is reunited under the Tang dynasty.
c.668 Korea is united by King Silla.
710 The Nara period, with the capital near modern Kyoto, begins in Japan.

794 The Emperor Kammu moves the capital of Japan from Nara to Heian (Kyoto).
c.890 Angkor becomes the capital of the Khmer empire in south-east Asia.

907 A golden age in China's history ends when rebellions and civil war destroy the Tang dynasty.
979 China is reunited by the Song dynasty, a great period for art and porcelain (left).
c.1020 The Cholas of south India invade Sri Lanka and Myanmar (Burma).
1044 Myanmar has its first national state.

AFRICA and MIDDLE EAST

622 Muhammad's flight to Medina (the *Hejira*) marks the first year of the Muslim calendar.
632 The Arabs invade the Near East.
641 The Arabs begin their conquests in North Africa.
696 Gold and silver coins minted in Damascus (right) feature verses from the Koran.
c.700 The rise of the West African empire of Ghana.

750 The Abbasid caliphate is founded at Baghdad.
760 Islamic scholars are using paper.
786 Harun ar-Rashid becomes caliph.
850 The Great Mosque at Samarra is built, with its spiral minaret (right). It is the largest mosque in Islam.
868 A Turkish dynasty is founded in Egypt.

c.900 Baghdad potters develop 'lustre ware', pottery with a metallic finish.
c.950 The earliest buildings are built at Zimbabwe.
969 The Fatimids gain power in Egypt and found Cairo.
970 Seljuk Turks enter the eastern regions of the Abbasid caliphate.

South America and most of Asia, civilisation developed under a series of ruling peoples or dynasties. In spite of sharp differences, life in all these regions depended on simple farming, and changes happened very slowly.

1050-1199

c.1100 Anasazi people build the great pueblo of Mesa Verde, Colorado, which includes a 'palace' with 230 rooms.

1200-1349

c.1200 The Aztecs settle in central Mexico.
c.1300 The Hohokam people are building multi-storey buildings, like this one, in Arizona (left).
c.1345 The Aztecs found their capital, Tenochtitlán.

1350-1499

c.1380 The Inca empire of Peru expands into central Chile.
c.1450 Taino villages on Hispaniola (right) have 1000-2000 inhabitants.
1492 Columbus arrives in the Caribbean.
1497 John Cabot reaches Newfoundland from England.

1054 The Eastern (Byzantine) and Western (Roman) Churches are divided for good.
1066 The Normans conquer England.
1073 The power struggle between the Pope and the Holy Roman Emperor begins.
c.1077 The Bayeux Tapestry (right), showing scenes from the Norman conquest of England, is completed.
1096 The First Crusade, a Christian invasion of Palestine, sets out.
c.1100 The first universities are founded.

1236 The Mongols begin their conquest of eastern Europe.
1282 Prince Llewelyn of Wales dies in battle, bringing the end of Welsh independence from England.
1314 The Scots defeat the English at Bannockburn.
1348 The Black Death reaches Europe.

1378 The 'Great Schism' begins in the Church (rival popes).
1389 The Ottoman Turks conquer south-east Europe.
1397 The Union of Kalmar unites the Scandinavian kingdoms.
1453 The Ottoman Turks capture Constantinople.
1479 Christian Spain is united under Ferdinand and Isabella.
1480 Ivan III ends Mongol domination in Russia.
1492 The last Muslim state in Spain falls to the Christians.
1494 The French invasion of Italy begins a struggle for power with the Habsburgs.

c.1090 The Ananda temple (right) is built in the city of Pagan, Myanmar.
c.1100 The temple of Angkor Wat is built in Cambodia.
1126 The Song dynasty is driven from northern China.
1192 The Kamakura period begins in Japan, and Chinese monks teach Zen Buddhism.

1206 The Delhi Sultanate is founded. The Mongol conquests begin under Genghis Khan.
1264 Kublai Khan founds the Yuan (Mongol) dynasty in China.
c.1275 Marco Polo arrives in China.
1338 The Ashikaga shogunate begins in Japan.

1368 The Ming dynasty is founded in China.
1398 Tamerlane captures Delhi.
1428 A Vietnamese state gains independence from China.
c.1434 The Khmer capital of Angkor is abandoned after Thai attacks.
1498 Portuguese ships arrive in India.

1055 The Seljuk Turks capture Baghdad.
1071 The Seljuk Turks defeat the Byzantines at the battle of Manzikert.
1076 The Almoravids of North Africa conquer the empire of Ghana.
1096 Christian crusaders invade the Near East and capture Jerusalem.
1147 The last Almoravid ruler in Morocco dies.
1171 Saladin conquers Egypt from the Fatimids.
1188 Saladin conquers the Crusader states in the Near East.

c.1200 The rise of the empire of Mali. Hausa states are established in northern Nigeria.
c.1250 The rise of Benin.
1260 The Mamelukes defeat the Mongols in Palestine.
c.1300 The art of glassmaking reaches its peak under the Mamelukes (left).
1300 The Yoruba of Ife make marvellous heads in clay, stone or bronze (right).

1352 Ibn Battuta, the Moroccan traveller, visits Mali.
c.1400 The stone citadel of Zimbabwe is built.
1402 Tamerlane defeats the Ottoman Turks.
1415 The Portuguese capture Ceuta in North Africa.
c.1450 The rise of the empire of Songhai in West Africa.
1488 The Portuguese reach the East African coast by rounding the Cape of Good Hope.

Who's Who

Al-Idrisi (1100-66), Arab traveller and geographer. He was born in Morocco and studied in many Islamic centres, but worked mainly at the Christian court of the Norman King Roger II of Sicily. His most famous work was a silver globe of the world. Idrisi's maps show that the Arabs had a much greater knowledge of the world than the Europeans.

Alfred the Great (849-899), king of Wessex. His was the only English kingdom not conquered by the Viking armies, and he agreed to let them have half England while he ruled the other half. Alfred was a good governor, lawmaker, and educator. His successors drove the Vikings out and became kings of all England.

Asoka (273-232 BC), grandson of Chandragupta and greatest of the Mauryan emperors of India. His empire included nearly all of modern India, Pakistan, Bangladesh and Afghanistan. He became a Buddhist, and his Buddhist inscriptions on rocks and pillars all over India are a valuable record for historians.

Bede (the Venerable Bede, 673-735), English monk and historian. For most of his life he lived in the monastery of Jarrow in Northumbria, the northernmost Anglo-Saxon kingdom. He wrote many books, but his most famous is the *History of the English Church and People*, the first history of England.

Saint Benedict (about 480-547), Italian monk, and founder of the Benedictine order. Living as a hermit, he gained many followers and started a monastery for them at Monte Cassino in Italy. The rules he wrote for his monks were copied in monasteries all over Europe, and no other order was founded until the 11th century.

Chandragupta Maurya (died 286 BC), Indian emperor, founder of the Mauryan dynasty. As a young man, he met Alexander the Great. He seized the throne of Magadha, destroyed the last Greek outposts in India, and built an empire in northern India and Afghanistan. He gave up his throne to his son in 298 BC.

Charlemagne (742-814), king of the Franks and emperor of the West. Success in war made him ruler of a large part of Europe, and in 800 the Pope crowned him as a new Roman emperor. His court at Aix-la-Chapelle (Aachen) was the main centre of art and learning in Europe.

Eric the Red (died about 1005), discoverer of Greenland. Born in Norway, he went to Iceland as a young man when his father was banished. When Eric in turn was banished from Iceland for three years, he went exploring. He discovered good land in Greenland, where he founded a colony. His son Leif sailed to North America.

Genghis Khan (1167-1227), Mongol conqueror. Son of a local chief, he was named Temujin. He was later called 'Genghis Khan', meaning 'world ruler', because after a long struggle, he united the Mongols and conquered a huge empire. His success resulted from good managment and, although he could not read, he was a good governor and law-maker.

Harun ar-Rashid (764-809), caliph of Baghdad. Under him the caliphate reached its greatest power and wealth. He made Baghdad the centre of Arabic learning, and was in contact with Charlemagne and Tang China. He led his armies to victory over the Byzantines. But, by his death, the power of the caliph was shrinking.

Kublai Khan (1215-94), founder of the Yuan or Mongol dynasty in China. In 1260 he completed the conquest of Sung China begun by his

grandfather, Genghis Khan. He understood and admired Chinese civilisation, and moved the Mongol capital from Karakorum to Beijing. The Yuan dynasty lasted until 1368.

Marco Polo (about 1254-1324), Italian traveller in Asia. He was only about 17 when he went to China with his uncles, who were merchants from Venice. He spent nearly 20 years in Kublai Khan's service,

travelling all over his empire. On his return to Italy he was imprisoned in Genoa, where a fellow prisoner wrote down his story.

Muhammad (570-632), founder of Islam. An orphan, he was brought up by an uncle, and as a young herdsman learned the customs and language of the nomadic Bedouin. After years of study and thought, he became a teacher and prophet. He was driven out of Mecca but welcomed in Medina and, after a civil war, he became the leader of all Arabia.

Otto I (912-973), German king. He was crowned Holy Roman Emperor by the Pope in 962, reviving the idea of a Christian, European empire begun by Charlemagne. With their main centre of power in Germany, there were Holy Roman Emperors in Europe from 962 until 1806.

Saladin (Salah ad-Din, 1138-93), Muslim commander against the Crusaders. After making himself ruler of Egypt and Syria, he led a holy war against the Crusaders, recapturing Jerusalem and defeating the efforts of the Third Crusade to get it back. He was also a good governor, restoring Egypt's power and wealth.

Shotoku Taishi (573-621), Japanese ruler. As regent for his aunt, the Empress, he strengthened the imperial government and reduced the powers of the nobles. He was in contact with Tang China, and introduced the Chinese system of government, including Confucian and Buddhist ideas.

Wu Zetian (624-705), the only woman emperor of China. When her husband, a Tang emperor, died, she locked up her son and took power herself (690). A born politician, she encouraged good government and the arts. But she was – and needed to be – ruthless, spying on her ministers and having her opponents murdered.

Sundjata Keita (about 1210-60), king of Mali. He founded the Mali Empire by creating a large kingdom among the Mande people of West Africa. A tolerant ruler, he controlled trade routes across the Sahara and the supplies of West African gold. He is remembered as a great hero.

Glossary

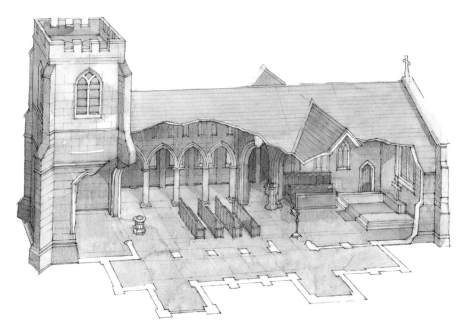

absolute ruler A king or other ruler whose power is not limited by laws.

Asia Minor The region of Asia nearest to Europe, roughly the same as modern Turkey.

calendar A system for dividing up the year into seasons, months and days, usually by the movements of the Sun and stars.

caliph The leader of Islam. As successor to Muhammad, the caliph was both ruler and religious head. The title became hereditary, but after 1258 no single caliph was recognised by all Muslims.

calligraphy Beautiful handwriting. It was one of the chief forms of art in ancient Egypt, in the monasteries of Europe, and in China and Japan.

caravan A group of traders, and sometimes other people, travelling in a group for safety. Traders in desert regions always travelled in caravans.

caste One of the strict classes into which people were divided, by birth and occupation, chiefly in India. Everyone was supposed to remain a member of the caste into which he or she was born.

civilisation A group of people who have reached a state of development that includes living in cities, organised government, a written language, fine arts and learning.

crusade A war waged with the support of the Pope for some Christian cause.

daimyo A member of the warrior nobility in Japan.

democracy A country or form of government where power depends on the votes of the people.

dictator A ruler with supreme power, above the law.

dissenters People who disagree with accepted laws or beliefs, especially in religion.

dynasty A ruling family, where the title is passed down from each ruler to his or her heir.

economy The management of the whole wealth of a state (or another type of community), including money, trade, and industry.

empire A state which also controls other peoples or states.

federal government The central government in a country made up of a number of states or provinces. The state governments control local matters, and the federal government controls national affairs, such as foreign policy and defence.

feudalism The way in which life was run in medieval times, especially in Europe. It depended on a bond between man and master. A man swore to work or fight for his master, in exchange for land.

finance The management of all money matters.

galley A type of ship driven mainly by oars, though some also had sails.

guilds Associations of merchants or craftsmen, which controlled much of the trade and business in medieval European towns.

hegira The journey of the Prophet Muhammad from Mecca to Medina in AD 622, the first year of the Muslim calendar.

hereditary title A title that is passed down in one family, from its holder to his or her heir.

heresy A religious belief that opposes the accepted beliefs of the time.

immigrants People who have settled in a foreign country, often because of persecution in their own country.

khan A hereditary king or ruler among the Mongols and other people of east-central Asia.

Glossary

knight A member of a class below the nobility but above the common people. In medieval Europe, knights were horse-riding warriors who wore armour.

legend A story that is probably based on true events.

mamelukes Meaning 'slaves', the royal bodyguards in Egypt who gained power as sultans from 1250 to 1570.

medieval period The Middle Ages in Europe.

mercenary A professional soldier, willing to fight for anyone who pays him.

merchant A person who lives by buying and selling goods. It usually means someone quite rich, more than a simple trader.

Middle Ages The period in Europe between the end of the Roman Empire and the Renaissance of the 15th century.

Middle East The region of south-west Asia from the Mediterranean to Afghanistan.

militia An armed force. Unlike an army, a militia is a local group of part-time soldiers, who are called up in an emergency, such as a rebellion.

monastery A community of people (monks) who live according to strict religious rules.

mosque A Muslim place of worship.

mutiny A rebellion by soldiers or sailors.

Near East The region around the eastern Mediterranean, sometimes including Egypt and south-east Europe.

nomads People who have no permanent home, but travel from place to place in different seasons. They raise animals but not crops.

patriotism A person's love of his or her country.

peasant The lowest class of country people, usually farm workers. Some peasants owned their own land. Others were serfs.

porcelain A very fine, hard type of pottery, which light will shine through. It was made in China 1,200 years ago, but in Europe only since the 18th century.

pottery Vases, cups, plates and other vessels made from clay and baked hard.

pueblo A village community living in a large building built of adobe (clay) or stone in what is now the south-western USA.

reliquary A precious box, often made with gold and jewels. It contained a holy relic, such as the bone of a saint.

rune stone A large stone slab with writing carved in letters called runes.

seal An instrument with a raised design for making a pattern in, for example, a clay tablet.

serf A person in the service of a lord, who 'owns' him or her. Serfs were not quite slaves, as they had some rights.

shogun The military governor, or ruler, of Japan from the 12th to 19th centuries.

shrine A holy place or building, such as the tomb of a saint, which pilgrims visit.

siege An attack on a castle or town defended by stone walls.

yurt A large tent made of felt on a wooden frame, the home of nomads in central Asia, including Mongols.

ziggurat A religious building like a pyramid, but with sides that rise in a series of steps.

Index

A

B

C

D

E

Index

Index

Index

Acknowledgements

Picture research by Caroline Wood

The publisher would like to thank the following for illustrations:

Julian Baker; p28t
Chris Brown; p11cr, p16-17b, p21b, p26-27
Tim Clarey; p32
Peter Connolly; p20b
Gino D'Achille; back cover, p30-31
Barbara Lofthouse; p14b
Olive Pearson; all maps
Robbie Polley; p22b, p23t
Martin Sanders; p13b

The publisher would like to thank the following for permission to use photographs:

Front Cover BAL "Kunstindustrimuseet; Oslo, Norway"; p8l Robert Harding, E.Simanor; p9bl Christie's Images; p9cr ET; p10t Werner Forman Archive, Courtesy Sotheby's London; p10b Werner Forman Archive, Beijing Museum; p12r Robert Harding, Gavin Hellier; p13t Werner Forman Archive, Kongo Nogakudo; p14l AKG photo, Jean-Louis Nou; p15tr ET, V&A; p16c MH, BM; p17t Magnum, Bruno Barbey; p17br Comstock, Georg Gerster; p18l AKG; p18-19 Photo Editions COMBIER-Macon; p19t"Ashmolean Museum, Oxford"; p19cr ET, "Bibliothèque Nationale, Paris"; p20tr ET; p23br ET; p24t "By permission of The British Library Ms.Stowe 17, f.89v."; p24b BAL, "British Library, London, UK"; p25t ET; p25b "By permissioin of The British Library Ms Roy 10.E.iv, f.65v"; p26tr BAL, "Fitzwilliam Museum, University of Cambridge, UK"; p27t BAL, "Vetrallaf Cathedral, Italy"; p28b BAL, Private Collection; p29 BAL, "Bibliothèque Nationale, Paris, France"

Key: BAL = Bridgeman Art Library; BM = The British Museum; V&A = Victoria & Albert Museum; ET = E.T. Archive; SPL = Science Photo Library;
      AKG = AKG London; MH = Michael Holford